Colonial America

Fun and Games in Colonial America

By Mark Thomas

Welcome
Books

Children's Press®
A Division of Scholastic Inc.
New York / Toronto / London / Auckland / Sydney
Mexico City / New Delhi / Hong Kong
Danbury, Connecticut

Photo Credits: Cover, pp. 7, 9, 17, 19 © Colonial Williamsburg Foundation; pp. 5, 13 © Richard T. Nowitz/Corbis; pp. 11, 15 © Kim Apley

Contributing Editor: Jennifer Silate
Book Design: Erica Clendening

Library of Congress Cataloging-in-Publication Data

Thomas, Mark, 1963–
    Fun and games in Colonial America / by Mark Thomas.
       p. cm. — (Colonial America)
    Includes index.
    Summary: Pictures and simple text describe some of the games played by children in Colonial America.
    ISBN 0-516-23935-X (lib. bdg.) — ISBN 0-516-23492-7 (pbk.)
    1. Games— United States—History—Juvenile literature. 2. United States—History—Colonial period, ca 1600–1775—Juvenile literature. [1. Games—History. 2. United States—History—Colonial period, ca. 1600–1775. 3. United States—Social life and customs—1600–1775.] I. Title. II. Colonial America (Children's Press)

GV1204.12 .T49 2002
790.1'922'097309032—dc21   9081
                              2001042357

Contents

Children in **Colonial America** played many games.

5

They played many **outdoor** games.

One outdoor game was called **rolling the hoop.**

7

Each child held a flat stick.

The child used the stick to roll a large hoop.

9

Children also liked to play a game called **nine pins.**

The players set up nine wooden pins.

Then, they rolled a wooden ball to knock down the pins.

13

Children also played
board games.

One board game was
called **Morris.**

It was played on a board
that looked like this.

Many children made their own toys.

Some children made dolls out of rags.

Children also played with toys made of wood.

19

Children in Colonial America had many fun games and toys.

21

New Words

Colonial America (kuh-**loh**-nee-uhl uh-**mer**-uh-kuh) the time before the United States became a country (1620–1780)

Morris (**mor**-uhs) a board game for two players; each player has nine pieces and tries to line them up in rows of three

nine pins (**nyn pihnz**) a game where players roll a wooden ball and try to knock down nine wooden pins

outdoor (**owt**-dor) being outside of a building

rolling the hoop (**rohl**-ihng **thuh hoop**) a game using a big wooden ring and a stick

To Find Out More

Books

Colonial Times from A to Z
by Bobbie Kalman
Crabtree Publishing

If You Lived in Colonial Times
by Ann McGovern
Scholastic Trade

Web Site
Old Sturbridge Village: Games, Quizzes, & Activities
http://www.osv.org/pages/gamesandquizzes.htm
Find out more about Colonial American children's games on this Web site. You can also play games like Morris.

Index

Colonial America, 4, 20

dolls, 16

Morris, 14

nine pins, 10

rolling the hoop, 6

toys, 16, 18, 20

wood, 18

About the Author

Mark Thomas has written more than fifty children's and young adult books. He writes and teaches in Florida.

Reading Consultants

Kris Flynn, Coordinator, Small School District Literacy, The San Diego County Office of Education

Shelly Forys, Certified Reading Recovery Specialist, W.J. Zahnow Elementary School, Waterloo, IL

Sue McAdams, Former President of the North Texas Reading Council of the IRA, and Early Literacy Consultant, Dallas, TX